A LOOK AT NATURE'S CYCLES

FOOD CHAINS
AND WEBS

BY BRAY JACOBSON

Gareth Stevens
PUBLISHING

CRASH COURSE

Please visit our website, www.garethstevens.com. For a free color catalog of all our
high-quality books, call toll free 1-800-542-2595 or fax 1-877-542-2596.

Library of Congress Cataloging-in-Publication Data

Names: Jacobson, Bray, author.
Title: Food chains and webs / Bray Jacobson.
Description: New York : Gareth Stevens Publishing, [2020] | Series: A look at
  nature's cycles | Includes index.
Identifiers: LCCN 2018039603| ISBN 9781538241066 (paperback) | ISBN
  9781538241080 (library bound) | ISBN 9781538241073 (6 pack)
Subjects: LCSH: Food chains (Ecology)--Juvenile literature.
Classification: LCC QH541.15.F66 J34 2020 | DDC 577/.16--dc23
LC record available at https://lccn.loc.gov/2018039603

First Edition

Published in 2020 by
Gareth Stevens Publishing
111 East 14th Street, Suite 349
New York, NY 10003

Copyright © 2020 Gareth Stevens Publishing

Designer: Sarah Liddell
Editor: Kristen Nelson

Photo credits: Cover, p. 1 (main) MZPHOTO.CZ/Shutterstock.com; cover, p. 1 (inset) Rudmer
Zwerver/Shutterstock.com; arrow background used throughout Inka1/Shutterstock.com;
p. 5 Igorsky/Shutterstock.com; p. 7 irin-k/Shutterstock.com; p. 9 Paul Reeves Photography/
Shutterstock.com; p. 11 (background) Rich Carey/Shutterstock.com; pp. 11 (food chain),
25 NoPainNoGain/Shutterstock.com; p. 13 Tony Baggett/Shutterstock.com; pp. 15, 21, 25,
30 (background) ismed_photography_SS/Shutterstock.com; p. 15 (food chain) Colin Hayes/
Shutterstock.com; p. 17 Andrew Astbury/Shutterstock.com; p. 19 alinabel/Shutterstock.com;
p. 21 (food web) snapgalleria/Shutterstock.com; p. 23 Derrick Hamrick/imageBROKER/
Getty Images; p. 27 Warut Prathaksithorn/Shutterstock.com; p. 29 ugurhan/E+/Getty Images;
p. 30 (food web) Vecton/Shutterstock.com.

Printed in the United States of America

CPSIA compliance information: Batch #CS19GS: For further information contact Gareth Stevens, New York, New York at 1-800-542-2595.

CONTENTS

Words in the glossary appear in **bold** type the first time they are used in the text.

IT'S ALL CONNECTED!

All the living things, or organisms, in an ecosystem are connected. Organisms have feeding **relationships** with one another, whether predator, prey, or plant. Food chains and food webs are the ways scientists show these relationships.

MAKE THE GRADE

An ecosystem is every living and nonliving thing found in a place, including animals, plants, and even the water and rocks there.

ON THE LEVEL

In food chains and food webs, organisms are grouped into trophic, or feeding, levels. Producers are often the first trophic level. They don't eat other organisms. Instead, producers make their own food. Most producers are autotrophs, which means they make their own food using **photosynthesis.**

MAKE THE GRADE

Common producers include grasses, flowering plants, **algae**, and some kinds of bacteria.

Consumers eat other organisms. The animals on the second feeding level are often called primary consumers because they eat producers. Primary consumers are commonly herbivores, which means they only eat plants. Others may eat algae or bacteria.

MAKE THE GRADE
Consumers are also called heterotrophs.

Secondary consumers are the animals that eat primary consumers! They're commonly carnivores, or meat eaters. Tertiary consumers eat secondary consumers and may eat primary consumers, too. There are also higher levels of consumers that eat the animals below them on the food chain!

MAKE THE GRADE

Top predators are animals that don't have any natural enemies. They're found in the highest levels of an ecosystem's food chain or web.

TOP
PREDATORS

TERTIARY
CONSUMERS

SECONDARY
CONSUMERS

PRIMARY
CONSUMERS

PRODUCERS

Decomposers are an important part of all ecosystems, but they aren't often shown in food chains or webs. Decomposers eat the matter from dead producers and consumers. They break it down into **nutrients**. These nutrients go back into the soil for producers to use!

MAKE THE GRADE

Common decomposers are bacteria and fungi,
as well as some bugs, slugs, and worms. They naturally
recycle matter in an ecosystem!

THE MAIN CHAIN

Food chains show how energy and nutrients move through living things as they eat and are eaten by other living things. Arrows between pictures of each organism show the direction the energy and nutrients are moving. Most food chains start with producers.

MAKE THE GRADE

Some food chains start with the dead matter of producers and consumers. They then show decomposers and detritivores, or consumers that eat dead matter.

ENERGY LOSS

Food chains and webs can only get so large. That's because living things use most of the energy they get from eating to stay alive. Not much of this energy is kept in their biomass, or body. And their body is what the next consumer eats!

MAKE THE GRADE

Some of what organisms eat cannot be **digested** and leaves the body as waste. That matter's energy is lost. It's not used or stored in the body.

Only about 10 percent of the energy that moves into a trophic level makes it to the consumers above it! So, the size of food chains and webs reach a limit. That's also why there are fewer consumers at the top of a food chain or web.

MAKE THE GRADE
Most food chains or webs can only reach about four trophic levels.

INTO THE WEB

The feeding relationships in an ecosystem aren't **linear** like a food chain shows. They're interconnected! One animal can be part of many food chains. A food web shows the feeding relationships between all the organisms in an ecosystem.

MAKE THE GRADE

The arrows in a food web point from an organism to the animal that eats it. One organism can have many arrows pointing to or away from it!

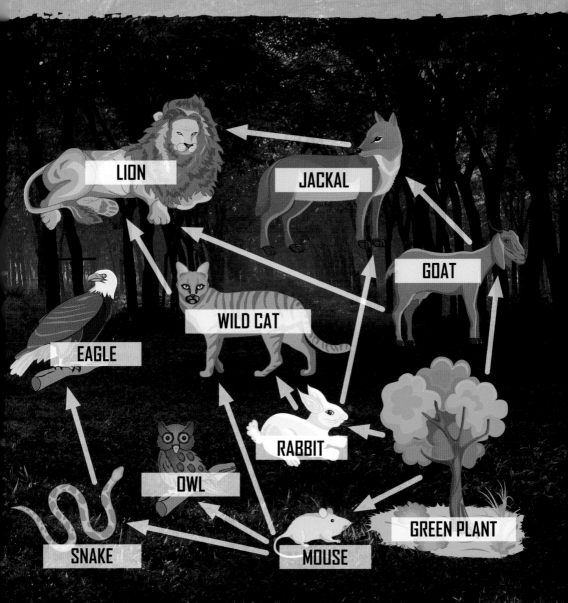

Food webs show that some organisms feed on more than one trophic level. For example, hawks, which are tertiary consumers, eat snakes, which are secondary consumers. But hawks also eat rabbits, which are primary consumers. Snakes also eat rabbits!

MAKE THE GRADE

Decomposers take part in the food chain at every trophic level! They break down producers and consumers after they die no matter what these organisms ate in life.

Some feeding relationships
are stronger than others.
When one organism
is the main source of
food for another, that's
a strong relationship.
When one organism is just
an **occasional** source of
food for another, it's a
weaker relationship.

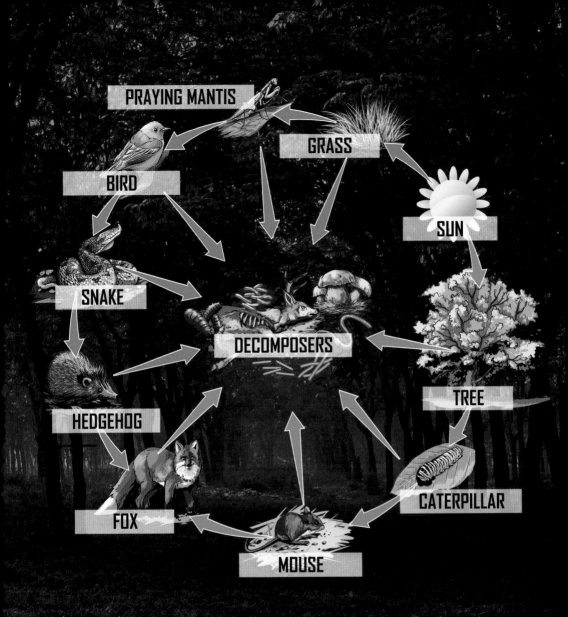

PRAYING MANTIS

GRASS

SUN

BIRD

SNAKE

DECOMPOSERS

TREE

HEDGEHOG

CATERPILLAR

FOX

MOUSE

MAKE THE GRADE

Food webs can look very much like a web. But that's
not the only way they can be drawn.

Food webs can help people study the effect feeding relationships have on the **population** of organisms. They can show which organisms **compete** for which kinds of food. They can show which animals are predators and which are prey.

MAKE THE GRADE

When an organism depends on a certain food, its population will decrease when the food disappears. This is more likely to happen if two organisms are competing for the same food.

PLACE FOR PEOPLE?

Every ecosystem has its own food chains and web. They can be simple and show just a few feeding relationships. Or, they can be **complex** enough to show many! People are part of the food chain, too. Where do you think we fit?

MAKE THE GRADE

In order for ecosystems to be healthy, they need a balance of producers, consumers, and decomposers.

29

WOODLAND FOOD WEB

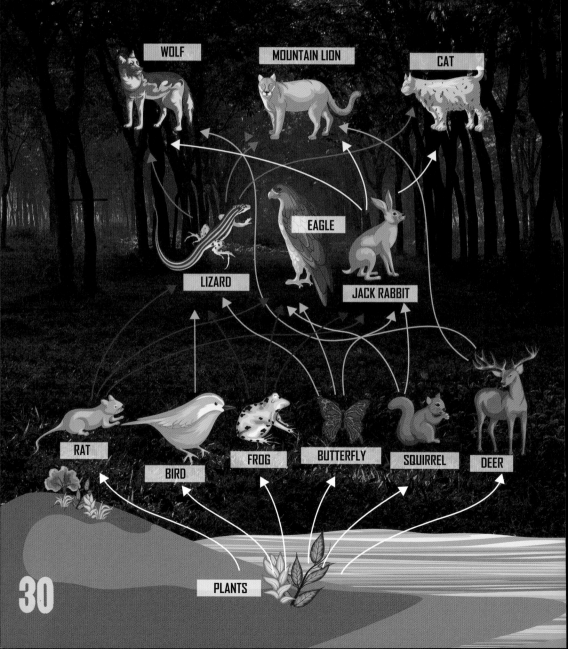

WOLF

MOUNTAIN LION

CAT

EAGLE

LIZARD

JACK RABBIT

RAT

BIRD

FROG

BUTTERFLY

SQUIRREL

DEER

PLANTS

GLOSSARY

algae: plantlike living things that are mostly found in water

compete: to try to be better or more successful than something else

complex: having to do with something with many parts that work together

digest: to break down food inside the body so that the body can use it

linear: going from one thing to the next in a direct way, as in a line

nutrient: something a living thing needs to grow and stay alive

occasional: happening or done sometimes but not often

photosynthesis: the process by which some living things turn water and carbon dioxide into food when exposed to light

population: the number of animals of the same kind that live in a place

relationship: a connection to another living thing

FOR MORE INFORMATION

BOOKS

James, Emily. *Do Monkeys Eat Marshmallows?: A Question and Answer Book About Animal Diets.* North Mankato, MN: Capstone Press, 2017.

Pettiford, Rebecca. *Rain Forest Food Chains: Who Eats What?* Minneapolis, MN: Pogo, 2016.

WEBSITES

Build a Food Chain
www.cserc.org/sierra-fun/games/build-food-chain/
Test your understanding of food chains and webs with this quiz.

The Food Chain
jmgkids.us/kids-zone/jmgkidsweb/natures-web/
Review the parts of a food chain and find an activity page.

Publisher's note to educators and parents: Our editors have carefully reviewed this website to ensure that it is suitable for students. Many websites change frequently, however, and we cannot guarantee that a site's future contents will continue to meet our high standards of quality and educational value. Be advised that students should be closely supervised whenever they access the internet.

INDEX